Ronald Campbell Macfie

Granite Dust : Fifty Poems

Ronald Campbell Macfie

Granite Dust : Fifty Poems

ISBN/EAN: 9783744718844

Printed in Europe, USA, Canada, Australia, Japan

Cover: Foto ©Thomas Meinert / pixelio.de

More available books at **www.hansebooks.com**

GRANITE DUST.

GRANITE DUST

FIFTY POEMS

BY

RONALD CAMPBELL MACFIE

LONDON
KEGAN PAUL, TRENCH, TRÜBNER & CO., Ltd.
PATERNOSTER HOUSE, CHARING CROSS ROAD
1892

[*The Rights of Translation and of Reproduction are reserved.*]

TO MY BEST FRIEND,

James Mathieson,

THESE POEMS

ARE LOVINGLY DEDICATED.

CONTENTS.

	PAGE
To James Mathieson	1
Alas, alas!	7
A Day in June	9
An October Eve	11
Kisses!	13
A Protest	15
God's Higher Education	17
Triumph	20
A Proposal	22
Verses	23
The Lyre	26
Song (Summer Wanes)	27
King Death	29
We Wail	31
Depart	33
With a Gift of Roses	35
Loveland	39
Caves	41
Fate	42
Harvest	44
The Shadow of a Cross	46
"A Pageantry of Mist"	48
Unattainable	49

CONTENTS.

	PAGE
Telemachus	51
Sonnet on Browning	53
A Face	54
Dragon Parable	55
That Night	56
White Heather	59
Nugæ Canoræ	60
ΠΡΟΣ ΚΕΝΤΡΑ	62
Why?	63
The Poet's Lyre	64
Parted	65
In the White Future	66
Pity	68
The Dying-Day of Death	69
Song (How will the Night)	73
Dawn	75
Never Again	77
Rondeau (Here Lieth Love)	78
A Polemic	79
Love Me	82
Hope	84
Two Sketches	86
No Saint	89
Hunger	90
Eyes	103
A Song	104
A Rosebud	105

GRANITE DUST.

TO JAMES MATHIESON.

Meseems it is a million moons ago
  Since first my eager life was launched from home.
The sky above is dark: the waves below
  Are white with foam.

But past the tempest and beyond the dark,
  Where evening sunlight falleth on the sea,
I watch the snowy wings that bear thy bark
  Away from me.

And now I can discern the empty sail
  Wearily flapping in the rosy west;
The sea around is calm: the homeward gale
  Is hushed to rest.

Thrice blessed, from such vantage to behold,
  Behind, the howling tempest, and before,
The crown of victory, the sea of gold,
  The eternal shore.

Now tarry, for thy toilsome days are done:
  Float like a weary sea-bird on the tide:
Thy wings and plumage by the setting sun
  All glorified.

Tarry a while—but why do we entreat?
  We know thee willing to prolong thy stay—
To linger when the air is cool and sweet
  At close of day.

TO JAMES MATHIESON.

Rather of God this mercy should we crave,
   More softly than an angel draweth breath,
May His wind waft thee o'er the western wave
   To life from death.

As in the vortex of a loving kiss
   May thy white soul to heaven be gently drawn,
And drift on slowly in a dream of bliss
   From dusk to dawn.

So softly and so gently mayst thou go
   Out of the sunlight to the land unseen,
That only doubtfully thy soul may know
   When death hath been.

So slow and peaceful may thy passing be,
   That we may ever keep, until we die,
A vision of thy sails upon the sea
   Against the sky.

That we may have thy semblance with us still,
    Lighting our voyage to the same fair goal,
And aiding us to bring as pure a will,
    As white a soul.

   .   .   .   .   .   .

Best friend, in voyaging, one early morn,
    Thro' surging mist that made me cold and blind,
My bark to a strange island-place was borne
    By wave and wind.

Dark desert-places I before had found;
    But this strange island was a happy spot;
Sweet-scented flowers blossomed all around,
    And withered not.

And I discovered, underneath the trees,
    With tattered garments and dishevelled hair,
A hundred haggard Sorrows on their knees
    In silent prayer.

And, standing where the sky was blue above,
  Maidens, with happy lips and earnest eyes,
Sang hymns of a divine undying love
  In Paradise.

And Memories, with patient widow-faces,
  Looked calmly backwards thro' the vanished years;
And smiled to find, like dew, in distant places,
  Forgotten tears.

And wide-eyed Hopes looked blindly on the world,
  Lost in great visions of a time to come,
When Falsehood should by Truth be Hellward hurled
  And stricken dumb.

Such was the isle yclept the Isle of Song.
  And I took freight of many songs and flowers
That haply, when the days were dark and long,
  Might speed the hours.

Now, friend beloved, tho' I cannot bring
  My songs and flowers to thy golden west,
Where only angels in the silence sing
  Anthems of rest ;

And tho' the distance make my voices vain,
  Yet to thy dear name do I dedicate
All I have won in voyaging the main—
  This songful freight.

SONG.

(Published in *Harper's Monthly*.)

Alas, alas, eheu !
That the sky is only blue,
  To gather from the grass
The rain and dew !

Alas ! that eyes are fair :
That tears may gather there
  Mist and the breath of sighs
From the marsh of care !

Alas, alas, eheu !
That we meet but to bid adieu :
  That the sands in Time's ancient glass
Are so swift and few !

Alas, alas, eheu !
That the heart is only true
    To gather, where false feet pass,
The thorn and rue !

A DAY IN JUNE.

The sun was zenith high. A lifeless cloud
    Lay in the west
Like a dead angel lying in a shroud,
    With lilies on her breast.

O'erladen was the shimmering air with balm
    And pollen-gold.
There reigned a perfect silence and a calm
    O'er hill and wold;

Save for the wind gasping among the trees,
    The gurgle of a spring,
The momentary sound of gossip-bees
    Low murmuring;

Or crackle of the ripe broom's purple pod
    Bursting apart,
Or song-bird palpitating up to God
    Singing its heart.

With light and butterfly the world did seem
    To flicker and flit
As though the Maker slept, and in a dream
    Imagined it.

AN OCTOBER EVE.

I.

THE dead leaves fall.
The air is cold and chill;
The world asleep and still.
The pine trees tall
In the dark wood
Stand brown and bare
In sunless solitude.
And everywhere
Reigns o'er the land a silence dread and drear,
O'er snow-capped barren hill and moor and mere.

II.

But, far away,
Borne in a breeze's wake
Thro' shaggy fern and brake,—
A stream's low·lay

Whispers along;
And now and then
A throstle's song
Comes down the glen,
Singing the dirges of the faded light,
And heralding the star-attended night.

KISSES.

White eyelids tremble on thine eyes,
    Dark lashes quiver on thy cheek;
Thy passive lips dispart with sighs,
    But never speak.

O love of mine, what thoughts hast thou?
    What thoughts make tumult in thy brain
When on thy mouth and hair and brow
    My kisses rain?

Is thought not trampled in the mire
    By passion's panic-eager feet?
What know'st thou but a face on fire
    With kisses sweet?

Are thoughts not dead? Nay, nay, they thrive;
   Lo, soul to soul we twain are brought
Intensely, wondrously alive
   In every thought.

The discords of chaotic hours
   Are linked in harmony at last;
The Present into crimson flowers
   Evolves the Past.

This is no mere corporeal bliss:
   No joy the grudging senses dole.
It is the hungry whirlwind kiss
   Of soul and soul.

A PROTEST.

WHAT temptress bodied of the devil's sighs,
    So termagant and tyrannous and strong,
As take thee from the flowers of Paradise—
    As bring thee from the banquet and the song,

To peer into the charnel-pits of Doubt:
    To waste the days in agony with Death?
God's mysteries are past all finding out.
    Life's joys are fugitive as human breath.

Because the ways of God are strange and dim
    Are other things inevitably vain?
Here is a goblet rosy to the brim
    Will wash cold sorrow from thy heart and brain.

And here are buttercups in gold attire,
  Daisies and daffodilies and heartsease;
And, fashioned of divine delicious fire,
  Red flower-lips more wonderful than these.

And night is glorified by moon and star;
  And day is gilded by its sun above.
Why fret and query what our destinies are
  When life is wonderful and God is Love?

GOD'S HIGHER EDUCATION.

As sunshine in the morning hours,
   Or pelting of an April rain,
Developeth the folded flowers
   And ripeneth the tender grain,

So He developeth thy mind
   So openeth thy folded heart:
By patient sun and rain and wind
   Persuading leaf and leaf apart.

.   .   .   .   .

The thought of other souls will fall
   With pregnant influence on thine;
And on thy leaves and petals all
   The light of holy lives will shine.

And Love will fan thee evermore
  With scented breezes from the South;
And Death will thrill thee to the core,
  Kissing thee with an icy mouth.

. . . . . .

Like lily-flower, like golden grain
  May thy soul thrive nor know the strife,
The feverish effort and the pain
  'This strange disease of modern life.'

Why vex thy soul with discontent?
  Wait passively as flowers do.
With every morning will be sent
  The silver sunbeams and the dew

Turn thy soul-chalice to the light,
  To the infinite blue above;
And God will make it fair and white
  And overbrim it with His love.

And they who watch thy soul increase,
   Its leaves grow white and strong and broad,
Will vaguely feel a holy peace,
   An effluence from the heart of God.

.   .   .   .   .   .

Not knowledge only, and book lore
   Will make thy spirit wise and good :
God's changeful summer more and more
   Must realize thy womanhood.

And in the autumn-time of death,
   When God doth make thine ignorance wise,
And takes from thee thy futile breath
   And gives thee spiritual eyes ;

Then thou shalt find thyself alone
   A naked soul of knowledge bare ;
For of it all canst only own
   What *in thyself* is good and fair.

TRIUMPH.

We triumph in the mere attempt.
    Thy blue eyes gleam !
At least our daring soul has dreamt
    A holy dream.

At least aspiring thought has flown
    Thro' starry space,
Has stood with God in heaven, alone
    And face to face.

And now altho' we must awake
    To the strife of day,
Must watch the frosty morning break
    Sombre and grey.

TRIUMPH.

A calm brow with an aureole
   Will aid our strife :
A secret vision in our soul
   Will hallow life.

A PROPOSAL.

TIMED by the rhythm of a languid strain,
   Leaning together in a waltz we turned;
   And a pent passion in my being burned
Till dumb endurance grew a very pain.
Yet I was silent, deeming speech in vain :
   Surely, as one in nether hell, I yearned,—
   Why should I climb to heaven to be spurned,
Why pray for what I never could attain ?

The music throbbed. Across my lips there swept
   A flame of hair. And then—I know not why—
But, seeing by her lashes that she wept,
   I dared my hopeless love to testify.
O God! against my side her heart upleapt
   In sudden, silent, passionate reply.

VERSES.

MAIDEN, thy life is like a morn in May,
    Holy and dim and sweet;
Thou wanderest along a dewy way
    With joyous feet.

Soft sunlight, slanting from an eastern hill,
    Burneth among thy hair.
Above thee all the welkin seems to thrill
    With praise and prayer.

Around thee in the woods the songsters sing
    Of love divine and deep;
Thy blood is salient with the soul of spring;
    Thy pulses leap.

Thou livest in the hundred harmonies
    That overflood the dells —
The humming of the honey-laden bees
    In heather bells,

The throstle's ecstasy, the blackbird's rune,
    The plover's plaintive cry,
The cricket-harper's melancholy tune,
    The breeze's sigh.

Thy world is half in blossom, half in bud,
    Lit by both moon and sun;
What joyance and what bliss are in thy blood,
    Thou happy one!

We lonely wanderers in wintry climes,
    Weary of frost and snow,
Gazing, have memories of golden times
    Long years ago.

Our winters vanish as we watch thee pass.
    Again the world is new.
The sun is in our eyes; and on the grass
    Twinkles the dew.

Again with dreams we glorify the dark
    That lingers on the sky;
In every cloud an angel or a lark
    Goes floating by.

Surely thy life is generous and true,
    If it can thuswise bring
Into sad days the freshness of the dew,
    The joy of Spring.

THE LYRE.

ʿΑ βάρβιτος δὲ χορδαῖς Ἔρωτα ἠχεῖ.

(Published in the *Academy*.)

SHE touched—and lo each silent silver wire
Won soul and music from her finger tips,
And trembled like some convent-maiden's lips
Pallid with holy passion and desire.
The evening shadows gathered; and the fire
Staggered and struggled with an unseen death.
Yet there I sat, and hushed, and held my breath,
To catch the palpitations of her lyre.

Wildly and witchingly the notes rang forth,
Charming alive the faces on the wall:
Meseemed I saw the warriors above
Wondering with the lyre what life was worth,
And acquiescing when the chorus call,
All tremulous with triumph, answered, "Love!"

SONG.

Summer wanes—I saw a swallow flying
  Southward in the search of love and light.
Sweetheart, hearken how the wind is sighing,
  Ever after blossom cometh blight.

Summer wanes—I found a lily lying
  Withered by the frost of yesternight.
Sweetheart mine, the roses are a-dying,
  Ever after blossom cometh blight.

Summer wanes—my lips are weary crying,
  " Love me a little when the sun is bright."
Even as I plead the echoes are replying,
  " Ever after blossom cometh blight."

Summer wanes—no longer, fate defying,
   Dally with Time, who is so swift of flight;
But place thy hand in mine and laugh, denying
   Ever after blossom cometh blight.

KING DEATH.

" Ha ! ha ! none dare marry me,"
    Chuckled the king called Death,
As, rattling his royal ribs together,
    He danced himself out of breath.

" Ha ! ha ! none dare marry me,"
    Sang he, thrumming his sickle :
" None of the women so wondrously fair,
    " Wondrously fair and fickle."

" Ha ! ha ! none dare marry me,"
    Chuckled the king of the scythe.
" Nathless, my beard is silky and long,
    " And my limbs are shapely and lithe."

"Ha! ha! I dare marry thee,"
 Laughed the maiden Love.
"I heard thy boast, and hastened here
 From the land of light above.

"Ha! ha! I dare marry thee:
 Even now we will wed."
And she kissed his brow, and his beard, and his eyes;
 And Death, as she kissed, fell dead.

WE WAIL.

We wail that the sky is grey
   And the silence wearily long.
The angels answer and say—
   " The God of your souls is strong.
Darkness hideth a day:
   Silence husheth a song."

We wail that our works may die
   And our sowing labour be vain.
The angels answering cry—
   " God, who rules the rain
And hangs the sun on high,
   Will surely tend the grain."

We wail we are weak of wing :
  That God is hard to find.
The angels answering sing—
  " Ah ! you are deaf and blind.
God is in everything :
  In and thro' and behind."

DEPART.

Was it a dream? Could God create
Of flesh and blood a thing so fair
With eyes so ignorant of care,
With brow so whitely delicate?
No dream I wot; and yet I swear
There seemed more soul than body there;
And mouth, and eyes, and hands, and hair
Seemed, in a spiritual state,
Immortal and immaculate.

No dream; and yet my waking sight
Saw never such pellucid eyes
So filled with peace of Paradise,
So lavish of a holy light.
No dream; and yet my spirit sighs,

And I would fain idealize
Thy loving glance, thy low replies,
And keep thy hand and forehead white
As holy dreams for day and night.

I fear lèst time or toil should mar—
I fear lest passion should debase
The delicacy of thy grace.
Depart, and I will throne thee far,
Will hide thee in a halcyon place
That hath an angel populace;
And ever in dreams will find thy face,
Where all things pure and perfect are,
Smiling upon me like a star.

WITH AN ANONYMOUS GIFT OF ROSES.

LISTEN, I lay these roses on thy path
    As petals by a summer wind are blown.
Why are thy gentle eyes so full of wrath?
    I, as a wind, am nameless and unknown,
And lost and hidden in a width of sky.
    What know you but a rose—a song—a sigh?

And would I were a wind, that I might claim
    A wind's invisible elusive flight,
And so might lay my heart on thine like flame,
    Or fly to thee upon some golden night,
All passionate and fragrant from the South,
    And crowd my soul upon thy crimson mouth.

Dream that I am a wind: then come and beat
    With thy white wings along my wind's demesne.
Innumerably on thy passing feet
    Wild kisses will be rained from lips unseen,
And hurricanes will toss thee to and fro,
    Like thistle-down or like a flake of snow.

Dream that I am a wind: then come and pass
    On pinion thro' the gentle loving air,
So gentle that it will not sway the grass,
    So loving it will swoon among thy hair.
Come, stretch thy holy wings, and glorify
    The clouds becalmed upon this breathless sky.

    .   .   .   .   .   .

Listen, I lay these roses in thy hand,
    As waves in some tumultuous moment lift
And lay salt sea-weed on the silver sand.
    Thou canst not scorn me, neither give me shrift;
For in the multitude I hide from thee,
    As waves moan back and mingle with the sea.

And would that I had Kharma in a wave;
    Then to thy feet my rising tide would bring
Red coral from some cold untrodden cave
    Where black leviathans are slumbering,
Or purple tangle like a mermaid's tresses,
    From desolate melodious wildernesses.

O dream I am a wave: then, thundering,
    My passion will make music in the surge;
Or tremulously, softly, slowly sing
    In ripples on the ocean's silver verge;
Or keep brave silence, and let shells alone
    Whisper its secret in an undertone.

Dream that I am a wave. O lady mine,
    O goddess mine, how I will flash the sun
Into the deepness of those eyes of thine!
    How I will gather moonbeams one by one,
And bind them in a heavy golden sheaf,
    And roll them to thee over rock and reef!

Is love so cheap? O lady, canst despise
  One who would stand and love thee from afar?
Finding his guerdon in thy happy eyes,
  Glorying in thee as in some white star?
Let me be to thee as a wind or wave:
  To sing about thy path is all I crave.

O lovely, scornful woman that thou art,
  Laughing into the shadow where I stand,
Rejoice that one should lay an unknown heart
  So absolutely in thy heedless hand:
Rejoice in my great unknown love, and wear
  These roses on thy breast and in thy hair.

LOVELAND.

Loveland, alas, has locusts,
    Pestilence and pain,
Storms that lay the lilies,
    Wind and rain

Marshes without a moon,
    Where black Death hangs and hovers,
Forests where bleach the bones
    Of poor blind lovers.

. . . . . .

Nay, nay, the lilies in loveland
    Never wither and die;
And locusts have never darkened
    Its azure sky.

These were not bones of lovers
 In yon dark dell:
Fool, you had lost your way;
 And that was—hell.

CAVES.

Caves are there, trodden by the sea alone,
   With labyrinths and mazes—long ago
   Silently sculptured by its secret flow—
Where crooked bones of uncouth beasts are strewn,
And hideous monsters lie and sleep, unknown
   Even to the waves that wander to and fro
   With eyes shut, fearing what their sight might show;
And trembling as they hear their echoed moan.

And every heart knows caves as dim and deep
   Where mouldy bones of uncouth sins decay,
With corners where old devils, half-asleep,
   Wait only for a voice or step to say
"Awake!" And full of awe we blindly creep
   From the deep darkness to the light of day.

FATE.

Spinning, spinning, spinning,
   She plieth her ancient loom;
Here, a silver beginning;
   There, a sable doom.
      The woof is shadow and sun;
   The warp, glory and gloom.
Spinning, spinning, spinning—
   Look how the shuttles run.

Spinning, spinning, spinning,
   She fingers the coloured thread:
And here a soul is winning;
   There a soul is dead.
      She mingles peace and strife:
   She ravels white and red.
Spinning, spinning, spinning,
   Webs of human life.

FATE.

Spinning, spinning, spinning,
   Discord mixed with song,
Suffering and sinning,
   Wills that are weak and strong.
   We think she worketh wrong.
   She seemeth old and blind;
Yet the web she is spinning
   God Himself designed.

HARVEST.

God, be merciful when he awaketh
    From his sleep.
God, be pitiful when he uptaketh
    His scythe to reap.

God, be merciful! Thou art his Maker.
    His life is vain.
Rampant weeds on every acre
    Have choked the grain.

Help him, God, Thou knowest all his weakness,
    Heart and hand.
Help him when he wakens to the bleakness
    Of his land.

Help him, God, in Thine own silent fashion,
    To arise,
Love and labour, till he find compassion
    In Thine eyes.

God, be merciful when he awaketh
    From his sleep.
God, be pitiful when he uptaketh
    His scythe to reap.

THE SHADOW OF A CROSS.

How far thro' space and time the soul may go !
  I had a dream as of a serpent's tongue
That darted venomously to and fro.
  I had a vision of the sword of flame
That guarded Eden when the world was young
  And shed a lurid light on Adam's shame.

I saw it animate with God's great Will,
  No hand was on the hilt to make it flash ;
Yet evermore its shriek, more piercing shrill
  Than a cicala's chirrup, clove the air ;
And all day long I saw it poise and dash
  A giant meteor with golden hair.

THE SHADOW OF A CROSS.

Firstly, I watched the morning-planet fade.
    The shadows on a yellow sky up-rolled ;
And, as in homage, the mysterious blade
    Cast crimson roses at a mountain's feet,
And turned a cloud into a cloth of gold,
    Where midnight and Aurora merge and meet.

And then I saw the drowsy birds awaken;
    And thro' their lilt I heard the meteor wail,
As wails a soul God's wrath has overtaken,
    As winds lament around a ruined keep,
As creaks a vessel's cordage in a gale
    When thunder walks upon the tortured deep.

Lastly, the Garden darkened and God came,
    Making a prayer of the discord shrill,
Hiding and sheathing in His light the flame :
    And lo,—decrepid with despair and loss,—
I saw swart Adam kneeling on a hill,
    To kiss the holy shadow of a cross.

"A PAGEANTRY OF MIST."

FLITTING and hovering in wanton flight
   Above a waterfall of foam and spray,
   The wind put forth a hand and filched away
A misty multitude of forms in white,
All bowing as repentant sinners might
   Confronted with the Resurrection-day—
   Only one moment were they given to pray,
Then dissipated to the Infinite.

And so, from out the foam of falling years
   The phantom of an olden memory
Is gathered by a wind, and re-appears,
   And floats with folded hands in prayer for me—
To vanish in a sudden rain of tears
   Down the dark distance of Eternity.

UNATTAINABLE.

Why cease to love thee? Is not loving free?
   I also love the daisies in the sod,
Discovering alike in them and thee
   The love of God.

And if I leave the daisies in the grass
   And thy bright beauty in thy Maker's care,
Why should I not sing softly as I pass,
   And call you fair?

I dare to love thee. Be it even so
   I also love the sunset in the west.
I find in thee and in the sunset-glow
   God manifest.

Why censure me? I would not rob the sky
  Of one red sunset rose or one white star.
And count thee unattainable and high
  As angels are.

My love is no mere passion to possess.
  I throne thee in a white exalted place,
And watch thy spirit's hidden holiness
  Transform thy face.

I crown thee with a sunny aureole,
  Acknowledging thy flesh is far from mine :
Only I dare to dream one day my soul
  Will gather thine.

TELEMACHUS.

I WILL be patient, tho' pent wrath and pain
    Catch back my breath :
Will hoard the tempest for a hurricane
    Of death.

I will be patient, tho' the blood may start
    To cheek and brow :
Will hide my hatred, saying to my heart
    " Not now ! "

I will be patient, tho' my mother's tears
    Bow me with shame :
Will stay to purge these black polluted years
    With flame.

For doubly fierce will lightning flashing free
Avenge our sorrow.
And doubly deep the pool of crimson be
To-morrow.

SONNET ON BROWNING.

How finished was his life, how strong and large!
   We have beholden him on passive wing
   A thousand various worlds pavilioning;
Anon, have seen him on a meadow marge,
Bent like a daffodil the dews surcharge;
   And lastly, we have watched him vanishing
   As silently and softly as the King
Who glided daywards on the dusky barge.

Death meant to such a soul no sudden change,
   No quick deliverance from sordid life;
     Alway his wings had been so brave and broad
That he would deem it nothing very strange
   To find within his arms an angel-wife
     Clad in the radiant holiness of God.

A FACE.

God's hand had made her face surpassing fair :
    In love had lingered over every line.
Its purity made Passion kneel in prayer ;
The starry eyes beneath the midnight hair
    Shone with a glory that was half divine.

Men, gazing, fancied that an aureole
    Circled the whiteness of her perfect brow ;
And a new discontent was in their soul,
For something holy from her presence stole,
    Drawing them nearer God, they knew not how.

THE SCIENTIFIC DRAGON PARABLE.

(With apologies to J. A. Symonds.)

THEY fable how the venom that a snake
    Once swallowed with a toad, gave growth and gain:
    How, by the torture of continual pain
It caused half-dormant faculties to wake,
And pinions with a gradual birth to break
    From the dark latency where they had lain,
    Until the serpent-lethargy was slain,
And a live dragon mimic wings could shake.

And whoso eateth of Sin's poisoned fruit
    Acquireth dragon-wings and dragon-breath,
    And dragon-like alive, alert may be.
Nathless, such wings are but a parachute
    To float him gently down the dark to death,
    A miserable black monstrosity.

THAT NIGHT.

THUNDER, with loosened limbs, lay huddled in a swoon.
Lightning had slunk away. There was never a stir in the air.
The trees stood statue-still as of motionless marble hewn,
Save one high branch that was bent before the moon,
By the corse of an Absalom wind hanging heavily by the hair.

Then my love took harp; and her fingers flashed on the golden strings:
Each hand like a living soul conscious and white and free:

Now fleet as flame, and prophetic of stormy, strenuous
   things,
Now impotently beating as beat the tortured wings
   Of a wounded gull outstretched on the wave of a
   golden sea.

Her bosom-tide went and came to its limits of pearls
   and lace,
   As surge might ebb and flow on a crescent of silver
   sand.
The moon moved thro' the clouds with even, passion-
   less face,
Throwing ivy-shadows like kisses on her face;
   And a brown moth came and hovered over her
   nimble hand.

O love, what a night was that! Why did I let thee
   go?
   Never was coward's sin so terribly accurst!

I left to the moon and the moth thy bosom's exquisite
  snow ;
And to-day I sit alone in the ashes of my woe,
  Withered, body and soul, with pain and famine an
  thirst.

WHITE HEATHER.

O QUEEN, I bring thee heather white as a prayer :
   Heather fostered beneath a German fir.
   But, hush, I hear a voice in the wind demur—
" Not white, but purple is meet for a queen to wear.
Bring purple heather for her royal hair,
   Or crimson heather—is not thy heart astir
   With a tumult of crimson blood when you think of
      her
So cold, so proud, and so surpassingly fair ? "

O queen, and I answer the wind in gentle-wise,
   Saying that I have chosen as embassy
This passionless heather, thinking it may devise
   Some white, soft, suppliant way toward my plea
To tell how earth is hallowed by thine eyes,
   How life grows holier in loving thee.

NUGÆ CANORÆ.

Hidden 'mong the forest trees
Chaunt thy liquid melodies
   Passionate nightingale!
Sing, till night's ten thousand eyes
   Fade and fail,
   Dim and pale,
As thou sang'st in Paradise
   Long ago.
   Sing in tender tremolo
   Soft and slow,
   Sad and low.
   Sing a deep adagio,
   For my heart is full of woe,

And mine eyes are full of tears
With the thought of bygone years
    Tremolo,
  Sad and slow.

ΠΡΟΣ ΚΕΝΤΡΑ ΛΑΚΤΙΖΩΝ?

Such fear as Jacob felt at Jabbok's ford,
  When all the livelong night his arms were locked
  About an unknown foe—whose patience mocked
His fiercest efforts—till like knotted cord
His temple veins were swoll'n, and till the sward
  Was trampled bare—even such fear as his
  My soul has felt, and in mine agonies
I tremble lest I wrestle with the Lord.

O thou strong wrestler, thou untiring foe,
Touch with thy death my sinews, make me know
  If thou be God who strivest thus with me.
Then as the weary Jacob, even so
  I will acknowledge and will worship Thee,
And, save thou bless me, never let Thee go.

WHY?

Lo! it is day; the land lies warm in light;
   The river ripples dreamily along
   Thro' golden meadows, listening the song
Of happy birds that, with unweary flight,
Dart o'er a sky immaculately bright:
   Thine arm is sinewy, thy heart is strong,
   Thy life is affluent and free from wrong,
Why wish to see beyond that mist-clad height?

Because the day will not for ever last,
   Nor will our winding way for ever lie
   Thro' sunny pasturage—because the sky
May momently with clouds be overcast—
Because when all these leas and lands are past,
   'Mong the mists yonder 'tis our doom to die.

THE POET'S LYRE.

The poet's song is sad : his cithern strings
    Are woven of the tresses of the dead.
This gold once fell upon a Dream's wide wings;
    And this was coiled upon Ideal's head;
And this fell languidly round Passion's throat,
    Down, down unto her billowy bosom-snow;
While that string lisping out so sad a note
    Made childhood beautiful an age ago.

Here are the locks of an unanswered Prayer,
    Hopeless and hungerful the words it saith;
And here a strand woven of Autumn's hair;
    While this belongéd to a languished Faith.
But listen how that string can plead and plain
    So the pale stars grow pitiful above.
Its strands are woven of a tress which Pain
    Kept from the coffin of a mother's Love.

PARTED.

Ah me! I cannot hear thy heart,
   Thy lips are pale with conscious lies;
Our souls have drifted far apart.
I cry, "O love, say where thou art,"
   And look for answer in thine eyes.

But lo, they coldly meet my gaze.
   Thou hidest thine emotions well.
Hast all forgotten olden days
And olden thoughts and loves and ways?
   Can this be thee, my Claribel?

Speak, for the sake of long ago.
   Draw near me for its dear sad sake.
This is not thee, my love: I know
Thy soul could never shun me so.
   Draw near me, or my heart will break.

IN THE WHITE FUTURE.

In the white future, in the coming years,
  We will forget our sorrow and our woe:
We will forget these death-extorted tears.
  Above yon open grave the turf will grow,
And flowers hide the failures and the fears
                    Of long ago.

In the white future, in the unborn days,
  Warm winds will steal the clouds that hide the sun.
Over the ruins roughening our ways,
  Lichen in green luxuriance will run,
And memory will only sing the praise
                    Of battles won.

IN THE WHITE FUTURE.

In the dim future, when the spray is blown
    From the near Jordan in our hair and eyes,
Shadows will show the stars that have been strewn
    Over blue heaven, till we realize
How there are things invisible, unknown,
                  Beyond the skies.

PITY.

O FOOLISH-HEARTED woman, trifler with love and life,
  Truly, I know not whether I scorn or pity or hate—
Only that wintry winds hold melancholy strife
  Round a temple's recent ruins and a garden desolate.

Scorn or pity or hate. Thine eyes are hard and cold.
  Surely thou needest pity, and shall I refuse thee mine?
O thou most miserable, who hast bartered love for gold,
  In loveless days remember my pity true is thine.

THE DYING-DAY OF DEATH.

I, who had slept the dreamless sleep of Death
    For æons, wakened to a sense of pain,
Wrenched my stiff hands asunder, gasped for breath,
    And was a man again.

The tatters of torn heaven overhead
    Were swayed by hurrying wings and busy breath.
It was the resurrection of the dead,
    The dying-day of Death.

The sun had halted half-way down the west;
    But in the shadow of the pendant blue,
Patient and calm amid the world's unrest,
    There shone a star or two.

Weird voices wailed about the vexed sea;
    Cold corses lay upon the yellow sands,
Panting themselves to life and painfully
    Moving their ashen hands.

And in a valley a black cloud was lying,
    Lifted by some great giant's moaning breath.
I dared to ask "Is that old Thunder dying?"
    One whispered—"Nay, but death."

Ev'n where I stood I heard him moan and gasp;
    Saw the cloud rising, falling like a sea;
And watched the hungry fingers pluck and grasp
    The rocks deliriously.

Then, moving onward for a little space,
    I climbed a hill, and on the plain below
Beheld astoniéd the hollow face
    Of man's relentless foe.

THE DYING-DAY OF DEATH.

About his temples, sinuous serpent veins
   Seemed writhing; and his lips were thin and
      starven;
While by the chisel of a myriad pains
   His great brow-dome was carven.

A broken scythe had fallen on the grass;
   I saw brown blood upon it from afar.
But one small corner was as bright as glass,
   And had a mirrored star.

So huge the blade, it might have formed an arch
   O'er Jordan; and the heavy handle leant
Its weight against a pluméd patriarch larch
   Until it bowed and bent.

Lo, as I looked, death's talon-fingers locked
   Convulsively; his hands were heart-wards pressed:
The whole land on a sudden rolled and rocked,
   Then lapséd into rest.

There lay God's grimmest, greatest servant Death.

There lay the old inexorable reaper,
Moanless and motionless, devoid of breath,
A cloud-enfolded sleeper.

SONG.

I.

How will the night
Take flight?
How will the bright
Daylight
Waken our sleep?
Will it dart or creep
To kiss away our dream?
Will its earliest gleam,
Zenith-high
In a cloudless sky,
Dazzle our eyes
With sudden surprise?

II

Ah, nay, 'twill hide
Inside
A dusky cloud,
To shroud
Its gleam and glare,
Blindingly fair,
'Twill hide itself beneath
The dusky cloud of death
And softly, slowly,
White and holy,
From shadow creep
To waken our sleep.

DAWN.

What paucity of life contents thy soul :
    A dearth of song, a poverty of light ;
    While, all around thee, dissonance and night,
Like a wild sea, reverberate and roll.
    Fold down thy coward wings, but we will go
To prove God's work harmonious and whole,—
To seek the love that is the source of grief,
    The light that shadoweth the world with woe ;
    And doubt that stabs thro' darkness like a thorn
Will blossom to a star of white belief ;
And holy star-time fugitive and brief
    Will brighten into morn.

I dream the shadow has a lucent core,
    I dream the discord will resolve in song ;
    And this wild battle with belligerent wrong,
This universal riot and uproar,
    Heard thro' a hush beholden from a height,
Will show their purpose as we upward soar.
Even now a silver-dusted wing of Dawn
    Pierces the tenebrous cocoon of Night ;
    And throbbing, palpitating far away
Comes music like an angel's orison.
Into the dark of doubt I must begone
    To meet the songful day.

NEVER AGAIN.

Death reaped my hope and love long, long ago,
  Stealing mine idol in his cruel wrath;
  And never more upon my life's hard path
Shall love spring forth in bloom. For tho' I know
The wounded tree in greater strength may grow,
  Blossoming bright again; and mown grass hath
  Often a richer, rarer aftermath,
With my sad life it never can be so.

The loosened tendril ne'er will coil again;
  The withered rose will never raise her head
To meet the kisses of the warmest rain
  That ever was from weeping heaven shed.
And so my heart, half-petulant with pain,
  Cries—"Speak no more of love, my love is dead."

RONDEAU.

"Here lieth love." Deep lettered on a stone
    Are these few words, but never name and date
    To say what heart would so commemorate
A dear dead love, or by what hand were strewn
The withered roses. Hither, thither blown,
    A willow's branches quiver with a freight
    Of melody that seems articulate;
But men who listen merely catch a moan—
        "Here lieth love."

Mine are the roses and the dead love there.
    But silence! breathe no names; it were not meet
That she should know love perished by despair
    Because her crimson lips were coldly sweet,
Because her face was passionlessly fair.
    Nay, rather let her laugh when winds repeat—
        "Here lieth love."

A POLEMIC.

Thinkest thou that thy dimples deceive us,
    O thou coquette?
Thou wilt lure us, love us, leave us,
    Laugh and forget.

Ah! what is that,
    My fair?
  —A redbreast—a rose—
Plumage for your hat—
    Petals for your hair
        You suppose—

Nay, but, coquette that thou art,
    Dost understand?—
It is my heart
    Thou hast in thy hand.

Now then, toss it away.
Hearts blossom every day.
There are many more that beat
About thy feet.
Take one!
Break one!

What does it matter?
Lovers will come and flatter,
Calling thee fair,
And will bear
A heart for thee to tatter
Or to wear.

But what dost thou give for these?
Thine own heart's ease?
Down there on thy knees!
  Thou hast bartered thine own heart's love,
    Thou hast taken Love's name in vain,
  And look in God's face above
    Thou never canst again!

A POLEMIC.

Hearts are thy playthings: is it not so,
    O coquette?
But when we get love we do not know
    The gift we get!

Hearts are thy playthings—here is mine!
    Why, thine eyes are wet!
Love is holy and divine,
    O coquette!

LOVE ME.

How long did the sun's round passionate mouth
    Kiss that rose's lips, I wonder?
How long did the amorous wind from the south
    Try to press her petals asunder?

How long did the honey bee flit to and fro
    Ere she threw her red vest apart
And showed a glory of gold and snow
    Hoarded beside her heart?

Longer far have I yearned for thy love
    And flown round thy folded blossom.
Will pity or passion never move
    The proud disdain of thy bosom?

LOVE ME.

Love me! I loved thee long ago:
  Love me! the land is sunny:
Love me! look, how the roses blow
  And the bees are gathering honey.

HOPE.

SEE her flutter and fly,
    Flapping her wings beside us,
    Telling what blisses betide us,
    Only that time may deride us
        By-and-by.

Watch her quiver and run,
    Telling of blossoms and blisses,
    Tempting with curtseys and kisses,
    Offering love and caresses,
        Summer and sun.

Known of yore as a lie,
> False in her charms and chatter,
> Yet she will flirt and flatter;
> And we will follow—(what matter
>> By-and-by!)

TWO SKETCHES.

I.

With dreamy eyes undimmed by care
And earnest mouth and dusky hair
More calm she is than halcyon air,

Upon a languorous night in June,
What time the scented breezes swoon,
And brown bats flit across the moon.

More pure she is than the petals white
That dimple the dark breasts of Night,
As tiny cherub-fingers might.

TWO SKETCHES.

And cinctured with simplicity
She moveth like the singing sea,
And wotteth not the melody

That followeth her fairy feet,
And maketh sad existence sweet
With echoes of her bosom-beat.

II.

We tremble at the words she saith,
And wonder her audacious breath
Defying Love, despising Death.

And yielding neither moan nor prayer
To appease the skeleton Despair,
Whose fingers rattle in her hair.

By weight of many woes unbowed,
Imperious and pale and proud,
She sitteth in a thunder-cloud.

And, peering thro' the purple mist,
Our 'wildered eyes behold her twist
The jagged lightning round her wrist.

NO SAINT.

SOMETIMES her mouth with deep regret
    Is grave, I know :
Sometimes her eyes with tears are wet
As a bedewèd violet,
    And overflow.
She has her human faults—and yet
    I love her so.

And have I therefore loved amiss
    And been unwise?
Nay, I have only deeper bliss :
I love her just because of this—
    Her sins and sighs;
And doubly tenderly I kiss
    Her mouth and eyes.

HUNGER.

The pain has maddened me. Thy sunken eyes
Bear witness to the cruel miseries
Of thirst and hunger aching on alway.
And I am drained of life-blood night and day
By clammy vampires of a cold remorse.
The vultures banqueting on yonder corse
Scent carrion already in my flesh,
And flap their wings and whet their beaks afresh,
O Zeus, this hunger and this thirst of mine!
I have gulped fire as one would swallow wine,
Thinking to rid me of perpetual pains
But now a poison gallops in my veins,
And vampires dangle from my aching heart.
O Zeus, good Zeus, if pitiful thou art,
Have pity on my weary, withered life;

HUNGER.

Tempt me no more with vanity and strife.
Methought that near the gods that day I stood,
When fevered furious with lust for blood—
Teeth grinning, sinews stiffened into brass—
I reddened all the daisies in the grass,
Spilling men's souls. Was ever sword so fierce
As my good blade that day to cut and pierce?
The giant Letus gashed me on the face:
I cried, "The gods of Hades give thee grace!"
And, with a lightning double-handed blow,
Cut thro' his hauberk to his heart below.
Ha! even as the sword-blade downward rang,
I can remember how a foeman sprang
And would have cut me to the crimson ground.
My blade was in the corse. The craven hound
Jeered as he struck me. In the blood he slipped.
His blade broke on my breastplate. Then I gripped
With both hands at his throat, and crushed the breath
Out at his mouth, until his eyes in death
Bulged from their sockets. Next, a dying fool,
As, to retrieve my sword, I stooped to pull,

Tore with his teeth my heel. Not long he bit,
I stamped upon his face and shattered it.
Gone was my pain. The curses of despair—
The singing of the arrows in the air—
Were sweet as music ; and the blood below
Was fairer than the rosiest afterglow
On the white summit of an Apennine.
Then came the night with revelling and wine.
They set upon my brow a gory wreath ;
We drank unto the gods of War and Death ;
Till in a heavy drunken sleep I lay
Nor wakened till the stars had gone away,
Save one that fainted in the yellow west.
Ah ! but that one was god-like in its rest,
So calm and passionless and white and pure.
I cowered in my tent, and washed the gore
Off breast and brow ; and, woe is me ! again
Knew the imperious, impatient pain.

TO MARS.

CURSES and moaning, clash and rattle
    Of sword and arrow on helm and shield!
My soul was drunken with lust of battle
    Till vision reeled:

Till vision reeled, and the world was red
    As the marsh of blood that my sword had made.
God of War! how the foe fell dead
    Beneath my blade!

God of War! but I served thee well
    With carnage; and yet I live accurst
By a hunger that makes my heart a hell,
    And by burning thirst.

Finding in battle no deliverance,
I turned to feed and feast my soul with dance
And song and rosy love among the flowers.
On silent summer nights, in fragrant bowers,—
When on the sea the wind, as in a swoon,
Was stretched asleep—I sat beneath the moon
And listened to the nightingale's melodious song.
Or thro' my halls fair women danced along
Voluptuously-bosomed, almond-eyed ;
And sang a hymn of love, and laughed, and sighed
And swayed like lilies in a Southern wind,
Until a sudden passion made me blind.

HYMN TO VENUS.

 O Queen of Love, my soul's desire
  Goddess divine,
  Thy mouth on mine
  Is sweet as wine
  And fierce as fire,
  Goddess divine,
  My soul's desire.

Such songs they sang; and all the midnight hours
Went dancing half-deliriously by
Thro' hot, unholy labyrinths of lust.
By a fierce fever raging in the flesh,
By a wild agitation of the blood
My soul was kindled into lurid flame;
 And for a moment its deep pain was lost;

But when the flame died out my soul was left
Doubly tormented.   Oh, what woe is mine!
What gnawing hunger and what burning thirst!
So day succeeded day in riotous round,
All vanity and fire and restless pain;
Till one March morning brought a man of stone
With passionless eagle eyes that pierced all things
And never wavered.   Weary of unrest,
I summoned him and asked him whence his calm.
He answered "Wisdom."   Then new hope was born.
I toiled like reaper in a harvest field
To heap my mind with sheaves of golden lore.
Day after day unrestingly I toiled;
But, maugre everything, my soul was sick,
Nor all the revelations of the stars
Could heal its sickness.   None the less I toiled
To win that peace of his; till, yesterday,
I heard a sound of wailing in my hall;
And when a woman at my elbow said—
" The man who had the face of stone is dead.
He slew himself because a vain amour

Had drawn him from his adamantine calm
And filled his passionless eyes with hungry pain;"
Then "Curses, curses upon life!" I cried,
"There is no peace in all this world for men,
Love, wisdom, war, are equally in vain.
Curses and curses on the cruel gods!
Nay, nay, meseems there are no gods at all."

And lo, as thus I cursed, a slave arose,
With eyes so deeply in their sockets sunk
Under a bloodless breadth of polished brow,
He seemed a wretched runaway from Death,
And robbed me, by his woe, of rising wrath.
Mournful as winds that wander over graves
To gather briny tear-drops from the grass
Sounded his hollow, melancholy voice;
While ever and anon a blue vein ran
Across his forehead like a startled snake;
And ever and anon there glimmered light
In his dark orbits, as if in a cave
A star should blossom and then die away.

"Truly," he said, "thy only god is Death;
Never grey ashes garnered in an urn
So cold and dead and impotent as thou.
Dost think thy soul will rest content with aught
But sure belief in an Almighty God?
Or dost thou think to find Him in the stars?
Lo! these are less to Him than summer dust
And eddy on His path, not ankle-high.
Can our soul-hunger ever be appeased?
Can God, the Infinite, be found at all,
When every faculty and every sense
Is fitted to the finite? God is not
A man, compact of mind and hands and eyes.
Mind is the product of a soul and brain,
Fast fettered by a hundred thousand laws;
And, lacking laws, becomes no longer mind;
While hands, however huge, are only hands,
Inept to juggle with a million stars;
And eyes are only almsmen of the sun,
Too weak to win the secrets of a soul.
And if God be not man, can mortal mind

Conceive His nature, and from suns and stars
Infer a Maker? Nay, meseemeth not;
His makings must be nothing to His might,
Yet even His makings baffle us to guess
What may have made them. Surely man himself
Is the highest thing whereof he may conceive:
The only thing that he may trust and love.
And man the mighty *Maker* cannot be.
Must our souls then despair and quit the quest,
And be consumed in a hot hell of thirst?
Nay, I espy a loophole to escape.
A perfect man were an imperfect God;
A perfect man could make no suns nor stars
Nor souls, and yet why should not mighty God
Be *partially* revealed in perfect man?
The same strong Spirit that inspires the sun
Might manifest His strength in human flesh,
Might move upon the level of our lives
And *partly* show Himself in deeds and words
Divinely perfect. (For I dare to hold
Manhood admits perfection, maugre laws

That limit and restrain it. See, this rose
Is perfect tho' it lacks the gift of song;
This lily tho' it wavers in the wind;
And manhood may be perfect tho' God's soul
Can only with the brain and hands and eyes
Accomplish limited and lawful things.)
Great God might be revealed in perfect man;
And in such partial revelation seen,
And in such perfect imperfection known,
Provisionally we might worship Him,
Beheld as in a torso.

                    "But you say
That there is no such torso of great God;
That manhood is the attribute of flesh,
The energizings of a brain-bound soul
Working with certain tools in certain ways,
While all the works of God deny the tools
And timid methods of humanity:
And God in nothing has been known as man.
Nay, nay, O King! now hearken and believe.

I said such torso *might* be : but behold
Such torso *has* been. God's eternal soul
Has entered and animated mortal flesh,
Has taken its limits, frailties and laws,
And brought Itself within the present scope
Of human comprehension, human love.
This knowable, lovable, visible God was Christ—
That Christ we crucified upon a cross.
No human soul had ever spoken so,
With such oracular authority,
With such a calm, original contempt
For falsehoods fashionable in the world.
Strange !—strange !—how strange that all we men
Thro' arduous centuries had failed to find
Truths that the life and words of Christ have shown
As bright and fair and certain as the sun.
By a supreme sincerity of thought,
He pierced into the spiritual verities
That lay around Him ; and His holy words
We recognize indisputably true.
The universal and conventional plan,

Whereon all gods were fashioned, has been shown
False and mistaken by His humble life,—
A life so different from the life we deemed
A God would lead, and yet in deed and word
God-like beyond the thoughts and dreams of men
In power and beauty. Ah! we know Him God;
We love Him; learn of Him; and, where He leads,
Willingly follow tho' it be to death.
' I am the Way, the Truth, the Life,' He said,
The only Way thro' Truth to perfect Life,
To love and knowledge of the God unseen.

" God is to us three Persons, yet one God.
As Christ, our souls may love and worship Him;
And by the love and worship grow alive
To God the Spirit; while God infinite,
Suggested by the Spirit and the Son,
And *partly* known in these, we love thro' faith."
So spake the slave, then vanished like a dream;
And none can tell me whither he has gone.
O Zeus! this hunger and this thirst of mine!

EYES.

Ah, sweet and fair, how bright thine eyes can be!
Like sunlight dancing on a sapphire sea,
They dazzle—ah, they dazzle, dazzle me.

Ah, sweet, be pitiful! Thy bright eyes gleam,
They thrill me thro' and thro', until I seem—
In some delirious, delicious dream—

To lose my lips among thy temple-hair.
Be pitiful, I pray thee, lady fair,
For such a dream is a disguised despair,

Who sometime will waylay me in the night
And strangle me—his fingers talon-tight,
His bony knuckles resolute and white.

Ah, sweet, be pitiful! So bright thine eyes can be,
As down to death to dazzle, dazzle me.

A SONG.

Ah, what a song was that! How piercingly passionate!
Was it a song or a soul? Surely her soul flew there,
Stronger and fleeter than flame, upward to heaven's gate—
Rosy with her lips, pure, and proud, and fair,
Crowned with golden stars, winged with eager prayer.

A ROSEBUD.

A ROSEBUD—waiting for sufficient sun
    To free it from its bondage—is my heart.
O bright eyes, shine on it till one by one
    The winter-wedded petals fall apart!

Not all the blandishment of azure skies
    To tempt it from its lethargy has power;
Only the summer in·thy sunny eyes
    Can make the folded rosebud burst in flower.

Not the most genial breezes of the South
    Can quicken it and make its leaves expand;
Only sweet kisses of thy crimson mouth,
    And warm caresses of thy lily hand.

O bright eyes, shine ! O sweet red lips, be kind !
O lily fingers, touch ! O fragrant breath,
Breathe on it like a warm delicious wind,
And save it from the cold Desire of Death.

In love or in compassion save the bud,
Else shut, and hard, and cold for evermore
O, lady, sting and stir its stagnant blood,
Laying a burning kiss within its core !

O, come, complete it to a perfect rose,
Setting it from its winter-fetters free ;
And every leaf unfolding will disclose
A passionate immortal love for thee.

www.ingramcontent.com/pod-product-compliance
Lightning Source LLC
Chambersburg PA
CBHW031402160426
43196CB00007B/858